GUITAR GUIDE TO LEFT-HANDED CHORDS

BY RIKKY ROOKSBY

HAL•LEONARD®

Contact us:
Hal Leonard
7777 West Bluemound Road
Milwaukee, WI 53213
Email: info@halleonard.com

In Europe, contact:
Hal Leonard Europe Limited
42 Wigmore Street
Marylebone, London, W1U 2RY
Email: info@halleonardeurope.com

In Australia, contact:
Hal Leonard Australia Pty. Ltd.
4 Lentara Court
Cheltenham, Victoria, 3192 Australia
Email: info@halleonard.com.au

Order No. AM970684
ISBN 0-7119-8901-X
This book © Copyright 2001 Wise Publications

Written and arranged by Rikky Rooksby.
Music processed by Digital Music Art.
Printed in the UK.

Visit Hal Leonard Online at
www.halleonard.com

INTRODUCTION

Playing the guitar can mean getting to grips with a number of techniques. Your picking hand learns to strum with a plectrum, play with fingers, or to use a plectrum and fingers. Your fretting hand learns to hold down single notes or chord shapes. The simplest approach to the guitar is to learn to strum chords, the art of rhythm guitar. There are many books of chord shapes available but the vast majority are aimed at right-handed players. This chord book is prepared specially for left-handers.

In this book you will find the chord shapes used in your favourite songs. Whether it's pop, rock, blues, or soul, here are all the chords you need!

HOW TO READ CHORD BOXES

The six vertical lines in each chord box represent the six **strings** of the guitar; for left-handers, the thickest string (E) is on the right.

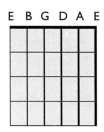

The horizontal lines represent the **frets** of the guitar. The thick horizontal line is the **nut** at the top of the neck.

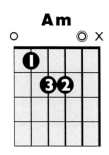

The **circles** on the fretboard show you where to put your fingers, and which fingers to put down.

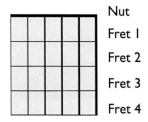

Numbers in a white circle indicate where the root note of the chord can be found. If the root note is on an open string, the 'o' is surrounded by another circle.

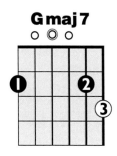

When shapes are played higher up the neck, the fret number of the **root** note of the chord is given next to the chord box.

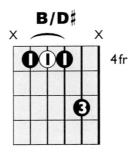

If a string is not played, an **x** appears at the top of the chord box above the relevant string. Open (unfretted) strings are indicated by an **o.**

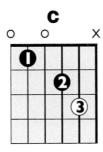

A **barre** is indicated by a curved line linking the strings to be fretted.

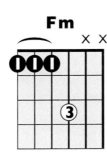

Example:

The chord box above tells you to:
- Fret the top three strings with your first finger at the first fret;
- Place your third finger on the third string at the third fret;
- Do not play the bottom two strings

It also tells you that the root note of the chord is **F**, found on the third string at the third fret.

MAJOR CHORDS

The most common chords are **majors**, and are used in all types of music. Here are 8 major chords – one for each key.

Note: there are two **G** chords – the second offers a slight difference in tone. **B** and **F** are a little more awkward than the other chords, so initially try these simplified shapes.

Here's a typical major chord progression:

A   C   D   E   A   G   A

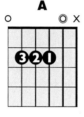

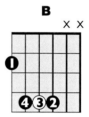

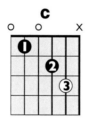

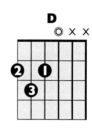

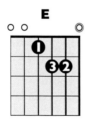

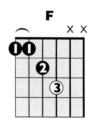

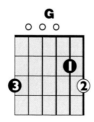

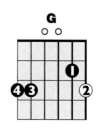

Sharp/Flat Major Chords

Here are the remaining five major chords on the sharp and flat notes. Two different ways of playing the **C♯/D♭** are given, one without a barre and one with. Try them both and use whichever feels more comfortable.

The two extra boxes for **B** and **F** give full barre moveable shapes. The position of the root note is marked by a white circle. Move the shape up or down until this note is the root of the chord you want. For example, if you move the **F** shape up to the 5th fret the note on the bottom string will be **A** and the chord will then become **A major**. As long as you keep the rest of the shape the same, wherever you move it on the neck will sound correct.

A♯/B♭

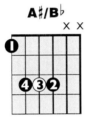

C♯/D♭

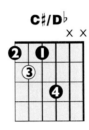

C♯/D♭

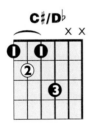

D♯/E♭

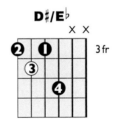

F♯/G♭

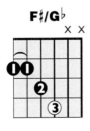

G♯/A♭

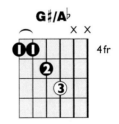

B

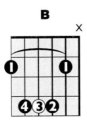

F

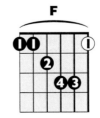

MINOR CHORDS

Here are the most commonly used **minor** chords.
Bm, **Cm**, **Fm** and **Gm** can be difficult at first, so
initially try the 'easy' forms below.

In comparison to major chords, minor chords sound
sad. Most songs use a mixture of majors and minors:

G   Bm   C   D   Em   Bm   Am   D

Am
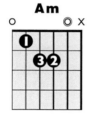

Bm
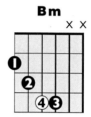

Cm
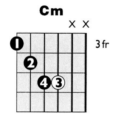

Dm
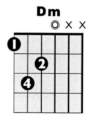

Em
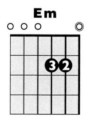

Fm
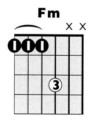

Gm
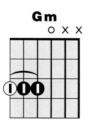

Gm
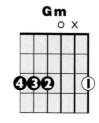

Sharp / Flat Minor Chords

Here are the sharp / flat minor chords. The two extra boxes (**Bm** and **Fm**) are moveable shapes. Compare these two barre chords with the **Bm** and **Fm** opposite, and you will see they are similar in shape. If you find the barre in the **F♯m** chord hard you can always lay your 2nd finger on top of the first to increase the pressure.

With these four shapes alone you can play 48 chords – the 12 majors in two different positions each, and the 12 minors in two positions each. Try this chord sequence to combine major chords with barred minors:

E   A   C♯m   A   F♯m   A   E

A♯m/B♭m

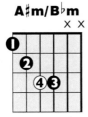

C♯m/D♭m

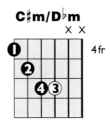

D♯m/E♭m

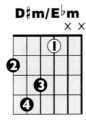

F♯m/G♭m

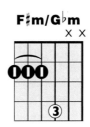

G♯m/A♭m

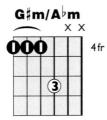

Bm

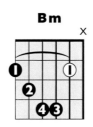

Fm

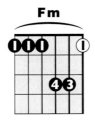

Bm(easy)

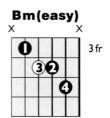

OPEN CHORD SHAPES

As we have just seen, a moveable chord (one that has no open strings in it) can be moved to create more chords of the same type, at a different pitch. But if you try to move an open string chord away from its normal position it becomes a different type of chord.

Often this results in something that sounds fairly hideous. However, sometimes it can create an appealing and exotic chord. Here are eight examples to delight your ear before we proceed with the next group of chords. Try this chord sequence:

C   D11   G   E♭   Dm7   C   G   D11

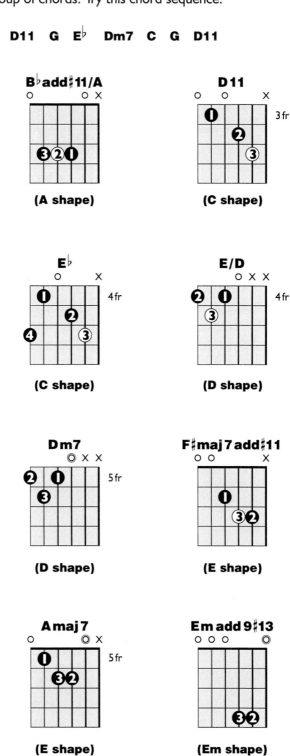

B♭add♯11/A
(A shape)

D11
(C shape)

E♭
(C shape)

E/D
(D shape)

Dm7
(D shape)

F♯maj7add♯11
(E shape)

Amaj7
(E shape)

Emadd9♯13
(Em shape)

1ST INVERSIONS

Emadd9♯13

Most guitar chords are known as 'root' position chords because the lowest note is the note after which the chord is named. If either of the other notes are at the bottom of the chord we get what is known as an **inversion**.

An A major chord uses the notes **A C♯ E**. If **A** is at the bottom we have a root position chord. But if we put **C♯** at the bottom we have a first inversion. (If we put **E** at the bottom, it's a second inversion.) These are notated with a '**slash**', the note after the slash being the bass note. Compared to a root chord, a first inversion sounds like it wants to go somewhere. Of these shapes the **D/F♯** and **G/B** are the most popular. With the **G/B** you can also leave the 4th finger off the 2nd string.

First inversions are often found in descending chord sequences:

A/C♯

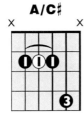

B♭/D

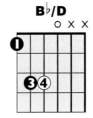

B/D♯

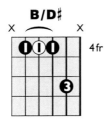

4 fr

C/E

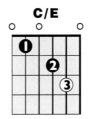

D♭/F

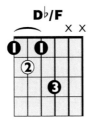

D/F♯

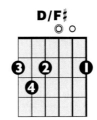

1ST INVERSIONS (cont.)

E/G♯
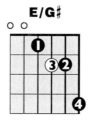

E/G♯
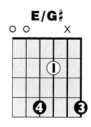

F/A
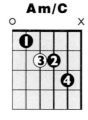

G/B
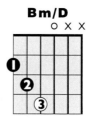

1ST INVERSION MINORS

G D/F♯ Em D C G/B Am D
You can invert minor chords as well, though these are less common. Here are four examples. If you only play the middle four strings of **Am/C** it becomes a moveable chord, as does **Dm/F**. Here's an example of how they sound:

Am/C
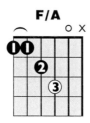

Bm/D
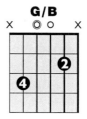

Dm/F
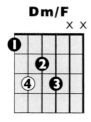

Em/G
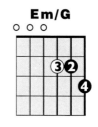

2ND INVERSIONS

G C♯ C/E Bm/D Am/C G/B Am G

Here are eight second inversion major chords. They don't sound as mobile as first inversions but they can be used in descending or ascending progressions. Try this one:

C G/B Am C/G B/F♯ Em

When playing the **B/F♯** let your first finger rest across the whole of the 2nd fret. Even though you only need

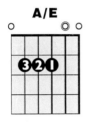

A/E

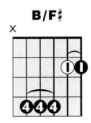

B/F♯

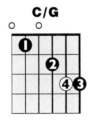

C/G

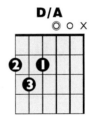

D/A

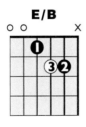

E/B

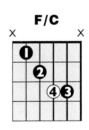

F/C

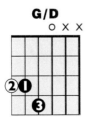

G/D

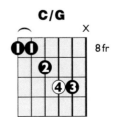

C/G

DOMINANT 7

the bottom two strings this makes for a more comfortable hand position.

After majors and minors the next important chord group is the dominant seventh.

Here are 12 dominant sevenths. Notice the contrast in sound between the two **A7**s and the two **E7**s. Use the last two boxes (**B7** and **F7**) as moveable shapes to find more dominant sevenths. The fourth finger on the **F7** is optional.

A7

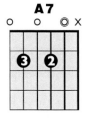

A7

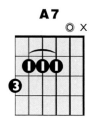

B7

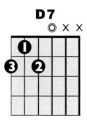

C7

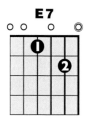

D7

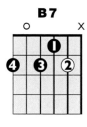

E7

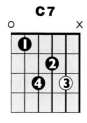

E7

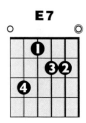

F7

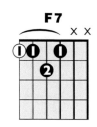

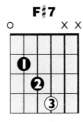

F♯7

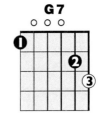

G7

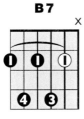

B7

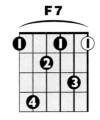

F7

MAJOR 7

TIP: If you find **B** an awkward chord to change to, try a **B7** instead.

Another popular chord is the major seventh. Here are 12 major sevenths (continued overleaf). Notice the contrast in sound between the two **Amaj7**s, the two **Emaj7**s, and the three **Gmaj7**s.

This is the result of the position of the seventh within the chord. Use the last two **Gmaj7**s and last **Bmaj7** as moveable shapes to find any major seventh you need.

Like the dominant seventh, the major seventh is a major chord but with a light, romantic quality. For this reason it is not used much in blues or rock but is vital for ballads and soul music. The major seventh will 'soften' a chord sequence, and works better at medium to slow tempos. Here's a sequence to try:

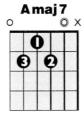

Amaj7

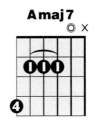

Amaj7

MAJOR 7 (cont.)

B maj 7

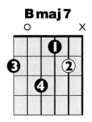

C maj 7

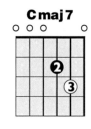

D maj 7

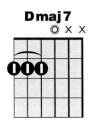

E maj 7

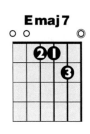

E maj 7

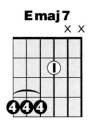

F maj 7

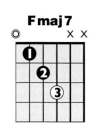

G maj 7

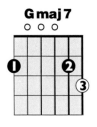

G maj 7

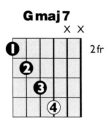

G maj 7

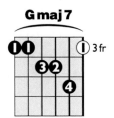

B maj 7

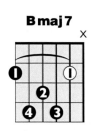

MINOR 7

A Amaj7 D Dmaj7 G Cmaj7 Fmaj7

Here are twelve minor sevenths. Notice the contrast in sound between the two **Am7**s and the two **Em7**s, where the second **Em7** has a stronger minor sound. Use the **Cm7** and the **Fm7** as moveable shapes to find some more minor sevenths.

The minor seven is a diluted form of the straight minor. If a progression seems too sad with minor chords, replace some of them with their minor seventh forms. The minor seventh is an adaptable chord, and occurs in most genres from folk-songs to hard rock. You can hear it in 'Father And Son'

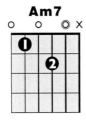

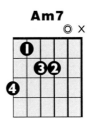

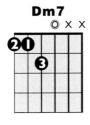

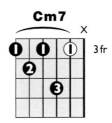

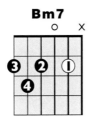

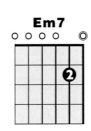

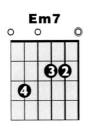

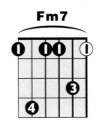

MINOR (MAJOR 7)

and Sting's 'Fragile'. Try this sequence:

Am7   Dm7   G   C   Em7   E7   Am
Here's an exotic type of minor seventh. The minor
(major 7) is formed by adding the seventh note of the
scale to a minor chord. In other words, it's like a
minor version of the major seventh chord. Its tense,
atmospheric sound is almost never used on its own
for more than a bar. You can hear it in The Beatles'
'Cry Baby Cry'.

Am(maj7)

Bm(maj7)

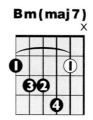

Cm(maj7)

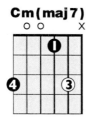

Dm(maj7)

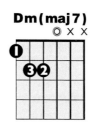

Em(maj7)

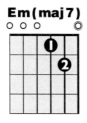

Gm(maj7)

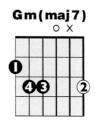

DIMINISHED 7

You will normally find it in this type of progression:

Am   Am(maj7)   Am7   D7   G
The diminished seventh chord is not very common outside jazz and it is neither minor nor major. It is made up of four minor 3rd intervals stacked on top of each other, so **Cdim7** would be: **C**, **E**♭, **G**♭, **A**.

I have provided two moveable examples here, covering all the keys you are likely to need. Here, any of the notes can be regarded as a potential root note, which is why the chord boxes have all those different names!

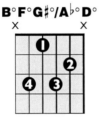

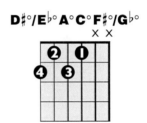

AUGMENTED CHORDS

The augmented chord is simply a major chord but with the fifth note raised by a semitone. **Caug** would be: **C**, **E**, **G**♯. You can hear the augmented chord in Led Zeppelin's 'Kashmir'.

Both diminished and augmented chords are usually found as passing chords between more ordinary root chords. Here's a sample chord progression:

G   A   D   D♯dim   E   D   Daug   Bm/D   D7   G

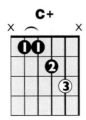

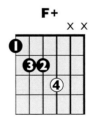

SIXTH

The diminished seventh can be heard in Meatloaf's 'I'd Do Anything For Love' and is also mainly used for key-changes.

Returning to major/minor tonality, we come to the **sixth** chord. Use the **C6** moveable shape to find any sixth you need. Notice the difference in tone between the two **G6**s.

The sixth chord is a light, summery chord found in pop, soul and jazz. If you strum the **E6** and lift the 4th finger on and off you will hear a classic rock'n'roll rhythm figure similar to that used by Grant Lee Buffalo on 'Fuzzy'.

A6

B6

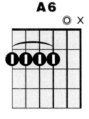

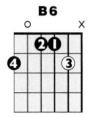

C6

D6

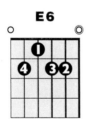

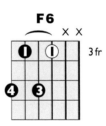

E6

F6

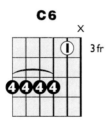

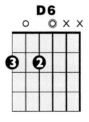

G6

G6

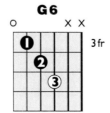

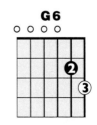

MINOR SIXTH

Here's a typical progression of sixths.

A6 D6 G6 C6 E E6 E E6
The minor sixth chord is harmonically similar to a dominant seventh. Notice that if you take your finger off the **D** string in the **Am6** shape you have **D7**.

There are eight minor sixths here – the **Cm6** and **F♯m6** are the moveable shapes.

The chord has an unsettled, edgy quality, and is used where a haunting or tense atmosphere is required. You'll hear it at the start of The Beatles' 'Happiness Is A Warm Gun', in Elvis Presley's 'Love Me Tender'

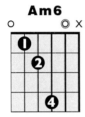

Am6

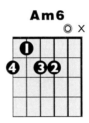

Am6

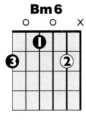

Bm6

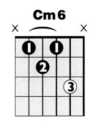

Cm6

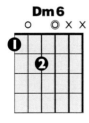

Dm6

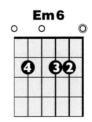

Em6

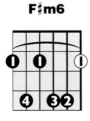

F♯m6

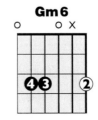

Gm6

FIFTH

and early in Radiohead's 'Paranoid Android'.

Em Em7 Em6 G Am Am6 D7 Em
Fifths are sometimes called '**power chords**'. They can literally be played with only two notes, but these shapes can also suit strumming. They have only two different notes in them, and so cannot be described as major or minor.

The fifth chord has a powerful, hard sound which makes it central to rock music. It is especially effective with distortion and/or at high volume. If you are playing with another guitarist try this progression with one guitar playing major or minor chords and the

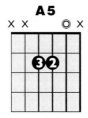

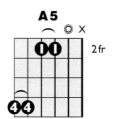

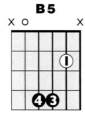

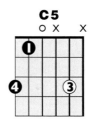

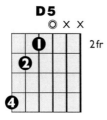

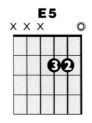

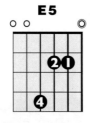

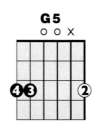

SUSPENDED 4TH

other the equivalent fifths:

G Em Am C D G G5 E5 A5 C5 D5 G5

Although it has three different notes, the suspended fourth chord is neither major nor minor. This is because the middle note is replaced with the fourth note of the scale. Use the **Bsus4** and the **Fsus4** moveable barre chords to find any others you need. The second **Asus4** box has a ringy 12-string sound. You can hear it on The Jam's album *All Mod Cons*.

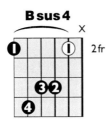

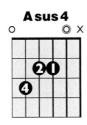
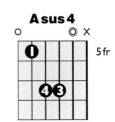

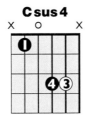
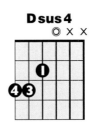

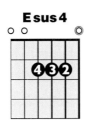
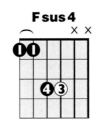

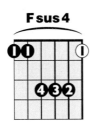
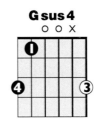

DOMINANT 7 SUS 4

Try this sequence:

A   Asus4   A   D   Dsus4   D   E   Esus4   Em
This is a variant on the suspended fourth. It is also neither major nor minor and can resolve to either. You can use the **B7sus4** and **F7sus4** as moveable shapes to find other **7sus4** chords.

Try this progression:

A7sus 4

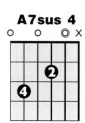

A7sus 4

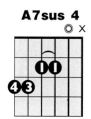

B7sus 4

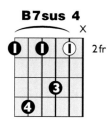

C7sus 4

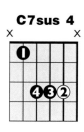

D7sus 4

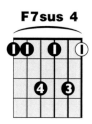

E7sus 4

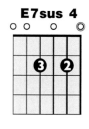

F7sus 4

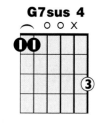

G7sus 4

SUSPENDED 2ND

E7sus4   E   E7sus4   Em
A7sus4   D   A7sus4   Dm
The suspended second is formed in a similar manner to the suspended fourth, by replacing the middle note of the chord, and so is also neither major nor minor. This time the middle note is replaced with the second note of the scale.

The **sus 2** is not as tense or dramatic as the **sus 4**. It has a slightly empty quality, making it good for slow, atmospheric ballads. You can also use it at quicker

A sus 2

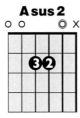

B sus 2

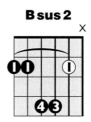

C sus 2

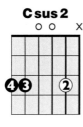

D sus 2

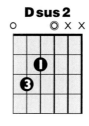

E sus 2

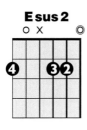

E sus 2

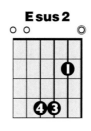

F sus 2

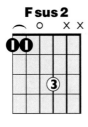

G sus 2

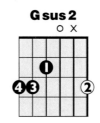

DOMINANT 9

tempos as a substitute for minor chords.

C Am Asus2 Dm Dsus2 G
This is an extended form of the dominant seventh. It is the most popular of the ninth chords, featuring in '50s rock'n'roll and '60s R'n'B. Its most famous use is in the funk of James Brown and a song like 'Rock Around The Clock'. The ninth softens the angularity of the dominant seventh.

If you have a progression of dominant sevenths try putting in a ninth:

A9
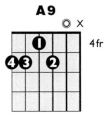

B9
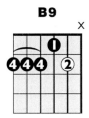

C9
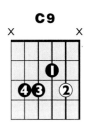

D9(no 3rd)
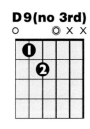

D9/F♯
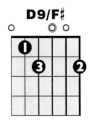

E9
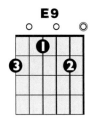

F9
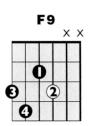

G9
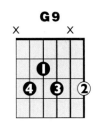

ADD 9

A7 A9 A7 A9 D9
D9 A9 E9 E9 A9

This is a straight major chord with a ninth added. The
difference between the **add9** and the **9** chord is that
the **add9** adds a ninth to a major chord, whereas the
9 adds a ninth to the dominant seventh chord.

It is quite popular in pop and rock, the ninth adding
extra colour to the major chord. It is similar to a **sus2**
chord but the difference is that it is definitely major.
You can hear the **add9** in 'Live Forever' by Oasis.

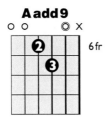

Aadd9

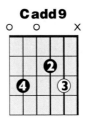

Cadd9

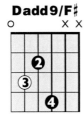

Dadd9/F#

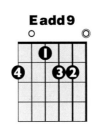

Eadd9

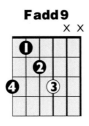

Fadd9

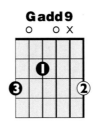

Gadd9

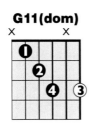

G11(dom)

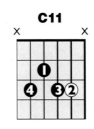

C11

MAJOR 9

Try this progression: **Cadd9**   **Dadd9**
G   **Gadd9**   **Fadd9**   **C**

This is formed by taking the **major7** chord and adding
the ninth on top. In this instance the ninth dilutes
some of the richness of the major seventh.
It is not as common as the other ninth chords.

Here's a progression to try:

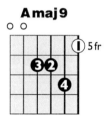

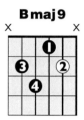

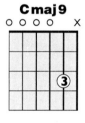

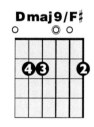

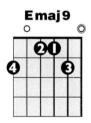

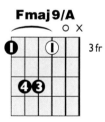

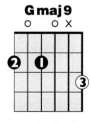

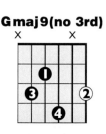

MAJOR 9/ MINOR ADD 9

C Cmaj9 F G C Cmaj9 F G

The minor chord can also turn into a ninth, either in the full form (**m9**) by adding the ninth note of the scale to the minor seventh, or as an **add 9** by adding the same note to the straight minor. Again, these types of chord are difficult to finger, and sometimes this means compromise is necessary.

Amadd9

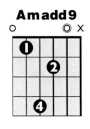

Amadd9

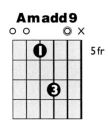

Am9

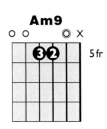

Am9

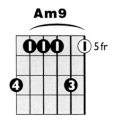

Bm9

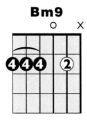

Cm9

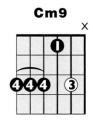

Dmadd9/F

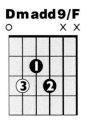

Em9

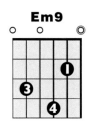

Gm9

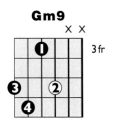

Dm9

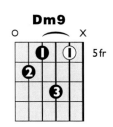

TIPS

Hopefully this book will have provided you with an easy reference guide to all the chords you use most often.

Here are a few more handy tips to help you when playing chords:

Guitar position

Make sure the guitar neck is always slightly above the horizontal. Never touch the neck with any part of the palm of the hand in an effort to exert pressure.

To increase your fingers' ability to stretch, keep your thumb roughly vertical but drop it down a little behind the neck. This will open out the hand. A low thumb position is vital when you play full barre chords.

Barre chords

Barre chords are quite hard so don't worry if you can't do them straight away. Check the 'action' on your guitar. This is the height of the strings from the fretboard. If the strings are too high barre chords will be difficult. A guitar repairer can reduce the action.

Try practising the barre chords **F** and **B** a few frets away from the nut. Roll the finger doing the barre – usually the first – so that you squeeze slightly to the right. The bonier edge of the finger is a better contact.

Clean chord sound

When you're strumming chords, make sure that all the notes that are supposed to sound do so. Check by striking each string in succession. Position your fingers near the fret to avoid buzzes. Check that adjacent strings are not accidentally muted by a finger catching them, and make sure you're pressing down hard on the strings. When each string resonates then play the whole chord.

FURTHER READING

If you've enjoyed this book, why not check out some of the other great titles suitable for your guitar case, available from all good music and book shops, or in case of difficulty, directly from Music Sales (see p2) or **www.musicroom.com**.

The Gig Bag Book Of Arpeggios For All Guitarists
AM946902
The ultimate arpeggio reference book for all guitarists, containing 240 arpeggios in all 12 keys. The handy fretboard diagrams illustrate the finger positions.

Tuning Your Guitar
AM35858
Easy-to-follow text and diagrams: will do wonders even for the so-called 'tone deaf'!

How To Use A Capo For Guitar
HLE00695255
Play with a capo in the style of The Beatles, Keith Richards, The Byrds and many more. An essential reference for all guitarists.

The Little Book Of Music Theory
AM954855
Introduction to the basics of music theory – accidentals, rhythm and time, major and minor keys, intervals, modes, scales, and chords, in one handy little book!

Left-Handed Guitar: The Complete Method
HLE00695247
Finally, a method solely devoted to lefties, complete with photos, diagrams, and grids designed especially for the left-handed player.

FURTHER READING

Gig Bag Book Of Guitar TAB Chords
AM943250
Over 2,100 chords for all guitarists, compiled by Mark Bridges and presented in unique guitar TAB format. Each diagram illustrates the fingering, inversion and notes of every chord.

Start Reading Music
AM80219
A proven, step-by-step method on mastering the basics of sight reading – whether you are an instrumentalist, singer or composer, this book tells you all you need to know.

300 Tips And Tricks For Guitar
AM945220
A practical guide for every guitarist. Includes choosing an instrument, reading music, chords and scales, blues, rock, jazz, country and funk riffs, and much more.

The Original Guitar Case Scale Book
AM76217
In this volume Peter Pickow gives guitarists a concise thesaurus of essential and practical forms for study and practice. Tips on using scales to build speed, endurance and fretboard fluency.

Basic Guitar Adjustments & Setups Pocket Guide
HLE00695149
An essential guide to guitar maintenance by John Boehnlein.